Complete BACH CELLO SUITES

Arranged for Plectrum-Style Guitar

ROB MACKILLOP

© 2022 by Mel Bay Publications, Inc. All Rights Reserved.
WWW.MELBAY.COM

Contents

Introduction 3

Cello Suite No. 1 (BWV 1007)
    Prelude 4
    Allemande 6
    Courante 8
    Sarabande 10
    Menuet I & II 11
    Gigue 13

Cello Suite No. 2 (BWV 1008)
    Prelude 14
    Allemande 16
    Courante 18
    Sarabande 20
    Menuet I & II 21
    Gigue 22

Cello Suite No. 3 (BWV 1009)
    Prelude 24
    Allemande 28
    Courante 30
    Sarabande 32
    Bourrée I & II 34
    Gigue 36

Cello Suite No. 4 (BWV 1010)
    Prelude 38
    Allemande 42
    Courante 44
    Sarabande 46
    Bourrée I & II 48
    Gigue 50

Cello Suite No. 5 (BWV 1011)
    Prelude 52
    Allemande 56
    Courante 58
    Sarabande 59
    Gavotte I & II 60
    Gigue 62

Cello Suite No. 6 (BWV 1012)
    Prelude 64
    Allemande 68
    Courante 70
    Sarabande 72
    Gavotte I & II 74
    Gigue 76

INTRODUCTION

Welcome to one of the greatest collections of solo instrumental music ever written.

Bach seems to have had a didactic plan for the sweep of the six suites, as each suite increases in technical difficulty as well as emotional depth. This is music that might well live with you for the much of your life, as it has for me. I first started playing these suites as a classical-guitar student some 30+ years ago, and have since played a variety of them on Baroque lute, theorbo, bass guitar, tenor banjo (see my Mel Bay edition: *Bach's Cello Suites I - III*, Mel Bay 30430M) and ukulele in 5ths tuning. Now it is the turn of the guitar (acoustic or electric) played with a pick or plectrum.

Pick playing – as with any technique – has its strengths and weaknesses. The pick gives incisiveness to pitch attack and rhythm, and can sound sweet or aggressive; all such qualities can be found in Bach's music, but sometimes this music requires the playing of two-note chords on non-adjacent strings. There are ways around this problem, however, which you should come to know:

1. Sometimes I have added a note in-between, if it seemed appropriate. For instance, between an F♯ on string 4 and a D on string 2, an A could be added on string 3, realizing a D major triad.
2. Sometimes it seemed more appropriate to mute one or more strings with the left hand. In the above example, the third finger of the fretting hand just needs to lean back a little to mute the third string.
3. Sometimes it is more appropriate to play the notes separately, especially in the slow sarabande movements.

Anyone who attempts to play Bach's music with a pick must learn to tackle these issues. In the early suites I have added a fair amount of left-hand fingering, but almost nothing at all for the final two suites. I suggest you work through the suites consecutively, as Bach no doubt intended; by the time you reach the 5th and 6th suites, you should be able to make your own decisions. And this is how it should be. You have to form your own relationship with this music, and that means analyzing the harmonic and melodic structures of each movement, and finding a way to best articulate that with both hands. Hopefully, you will grow in confidence as you work through the suites, but don't be surprised if in years to come you return to a suite and completely refinger it! This happens. We grow as human beings and musicians, and this music will always be there for us to wrestle with. I can assure you, this music is never the same twice.

The Baroque suite is a collection of dances in one key, and that key is first explored in a prelude. Bach tends to start simply, exploring the tonic, sub dominant and dominant chords of the key, before heading off the to "visit the relatives", often the relative major or minor versions of these chords, before heading home. As such, each prelude should be seen as a journey or adventure from Home to Away, back to Home again. Once we have explored the key through the prelude, we then proceed to further explore the key in the rhythmical context of a variety of dances.

The allemande is in 4/4, and often moves at a stately pace. Try to let the music unfold at its own pace, without rushing. There then follows a courante in 3/4 time. There are two types of courante, French and Italian. The former tends to be rhythmically quite complex, at a medium pace, while the latter is a fast-flowing uninterrupted flurry of 8th or 16th notes. There follows the sarabande – the emotional heart of the suite – where deep emotions are explored. Bach's sarabandes are always a high point within the suite. Look out for a subtle accent on the second beat of the bar – not always present, but usually felt. Then we have a more playful dance: either a menuet, bourrée or gavotte. These melodious dances arouse us from the deeply contemplative mood of the sarabande, and prepare us for the breathlessness of the gigue.

So, best wishes for your journey into Bach's cello suites! I've chosen keys which serve the music well on the guitar. Take your time, this great music will be around forever.

Rob Mackillop, Edinburgh, 2020

Cello Suite No. 1
Prelude

Arranged for plectrum guitar
by Rob MacKillop

J. S. Bach

Allemande

Arranged for plectrum guitar
by Rob MacKillop

J. S. Bach

Courante

Arranged for plectrum guitar
by Rob MacKillop

J. S. Bach

Sarabande

Arranged for plectrum guitar
by Rob MacKillop

J. S. Bach

Menuet I & II

Arranged for plectrum guitar
by Rob MacKillop

J. S. Bach

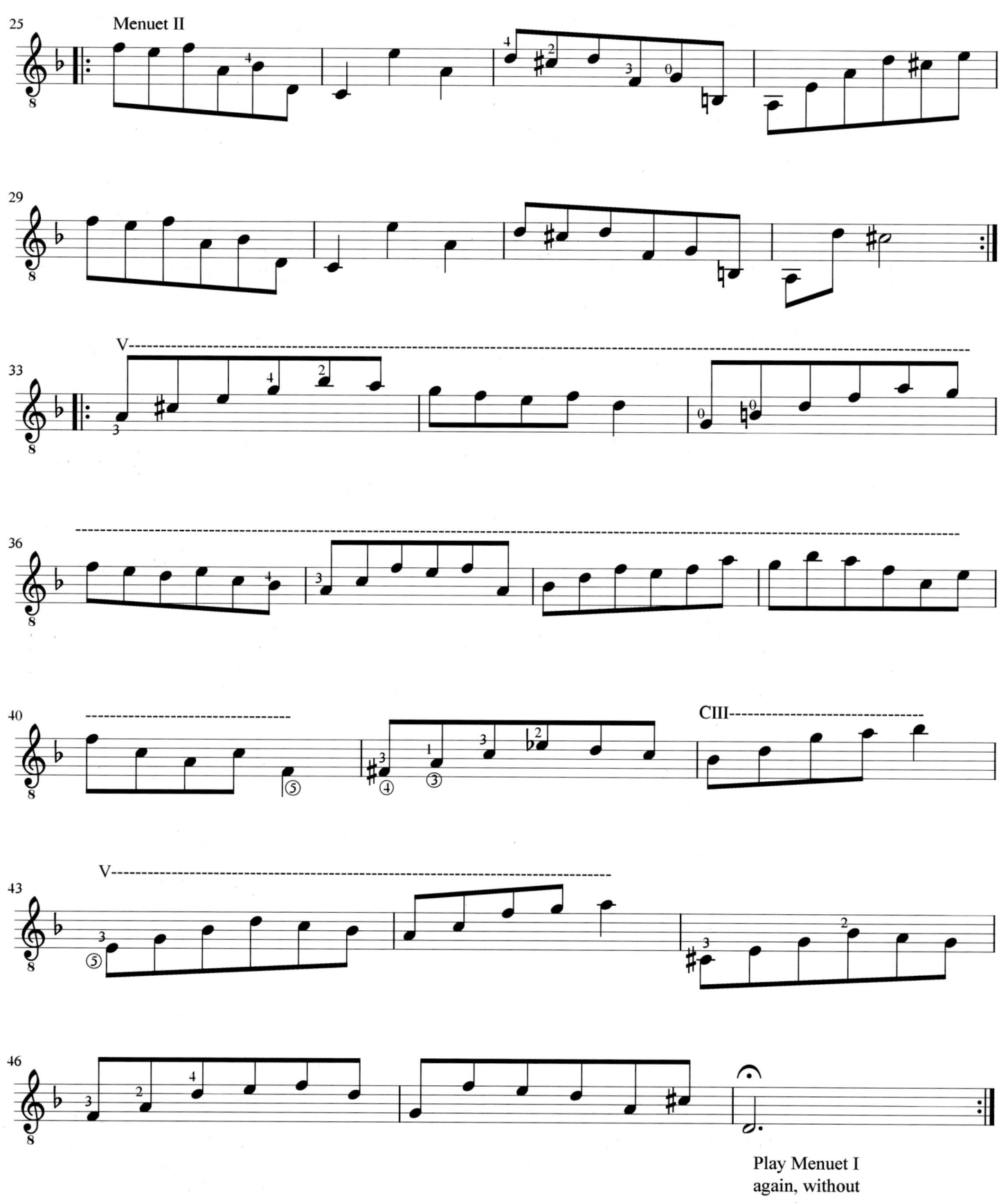

Play Menuet I again, without repeats.

Gigue

Arranged for plectrum guitar
by Rob MacKillop

J. S. Bach

Cello Suite No. 2
Prelude

Arranged for plectrum guitar
by Rob MacKillop

J. S. Bach

Allemande

Arranged for plectrum guitar
by Rob MacKillop

J. S. Bach

Courante

Arranged for plectrum guitar
by Rob MacKillop

J. S. Bach

Sarabande

Arranged for plectrum guitar
by Rob MacKillop

J. S. Bach

Menuet I & II

Arranged for plectrum guitar
by Rob MacKillop

J. S. Bach

Play Menuet I
again, without
repeats.

Gigue

Arranged for plectrum guitar
by Rob MacKillop

J. S. Bach

Cello Suite No. 3
Prelude

Arranged for plectrum guitar
by Rob MacKillop

J. S. Bach

This page has been left blank to avoid an awkward page turn.

Allemande

Arranged for plectrum guitar
by Rob MacKillop

J. S. Bach

Courante

Arranged for plectrum guitar
by Rob MacKillop

J. S. Bach

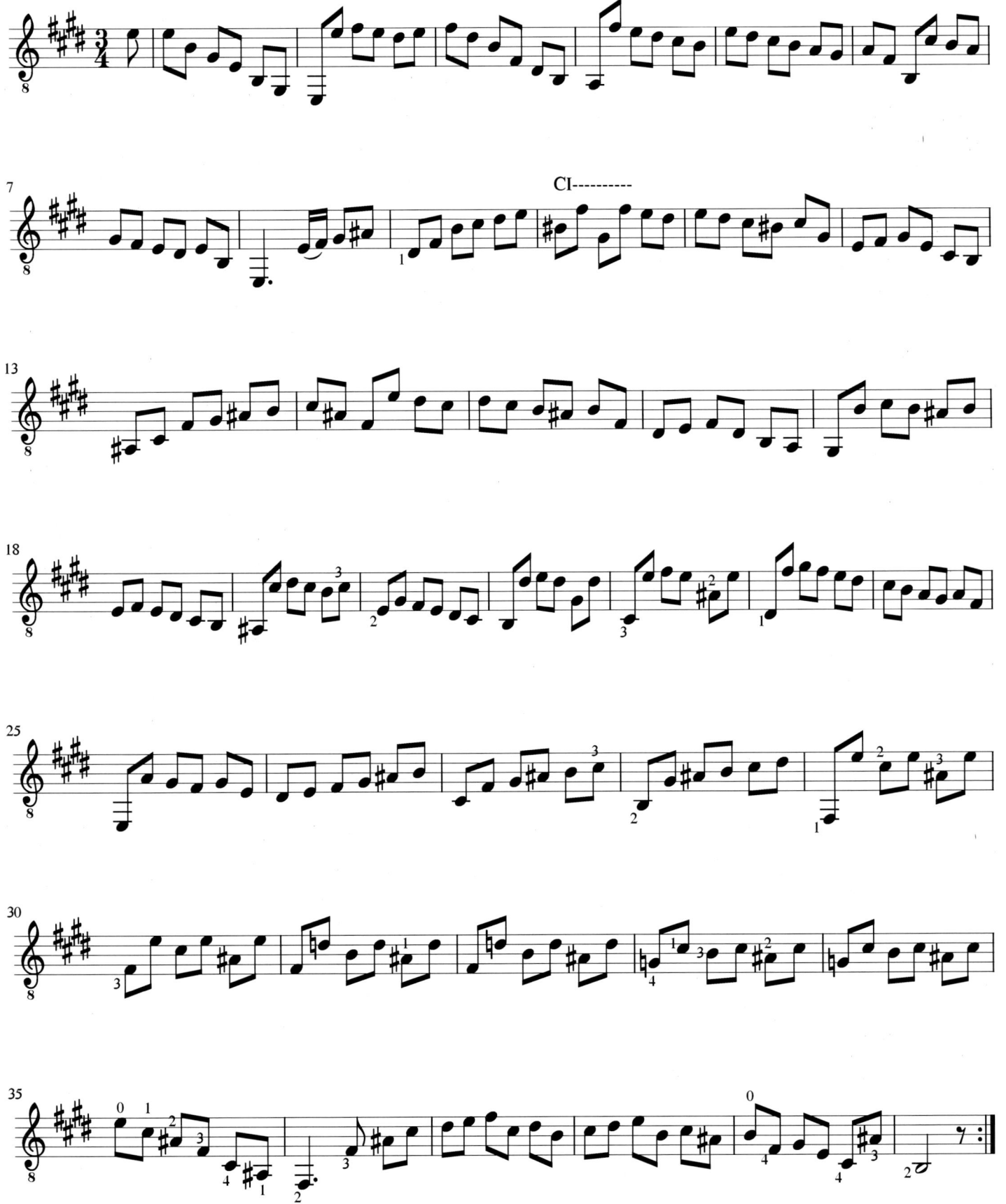

30

Sarabande

Arranged for plectrum guitar
by Rob MacKillop

J. S. Bach

This page has been left blank to avoid an awkward page turn.

Bourrée I & II

Arranged for plectrum guitar
by Rob MacKillop

J. S. Bach

Gigue

Arranged for plectrum guitar
by Rob MacKillop

J. S. Bach

Cello Suite No. 4
Prelude

Arranged for plectrum guitar
by Rob MacKillop

J. S. Bach

This page has been left blank to avoid an awkward page turn.

Allemande

Arranged for plectrum guitar
by Rob MacKillop

J. S. Bach

Courante

Arranged for plectrum guitar
by Rob MacKillop

J. S. Bach

Sarabande

Arranged for plectrum guitar
by Rob MacKillop

J. S. Bach

This page has been left blank to avoid an awkward page turn.

Bourrée I & II

Arranged for plectrum guitar
by Rob MacKillop

J. S. Bach

Gigue

Arranged for plectrum guitar
by Rob MacKillop

J. S. Bach

Cello Suite No. 5
Prelude

Arranged for plectrum guitar
by Rob MacKillop

J. S. Bach

Allemande

Arranged for plectrum guitar
by Rob MacKillop

J. S. Bach

Courante

Arranged for plectrum guitar
by Rob MacKillop

J. S. Bach

Sarabande

Arranged for plectrum guitar
by Rob MacKillop

J. S. Bach

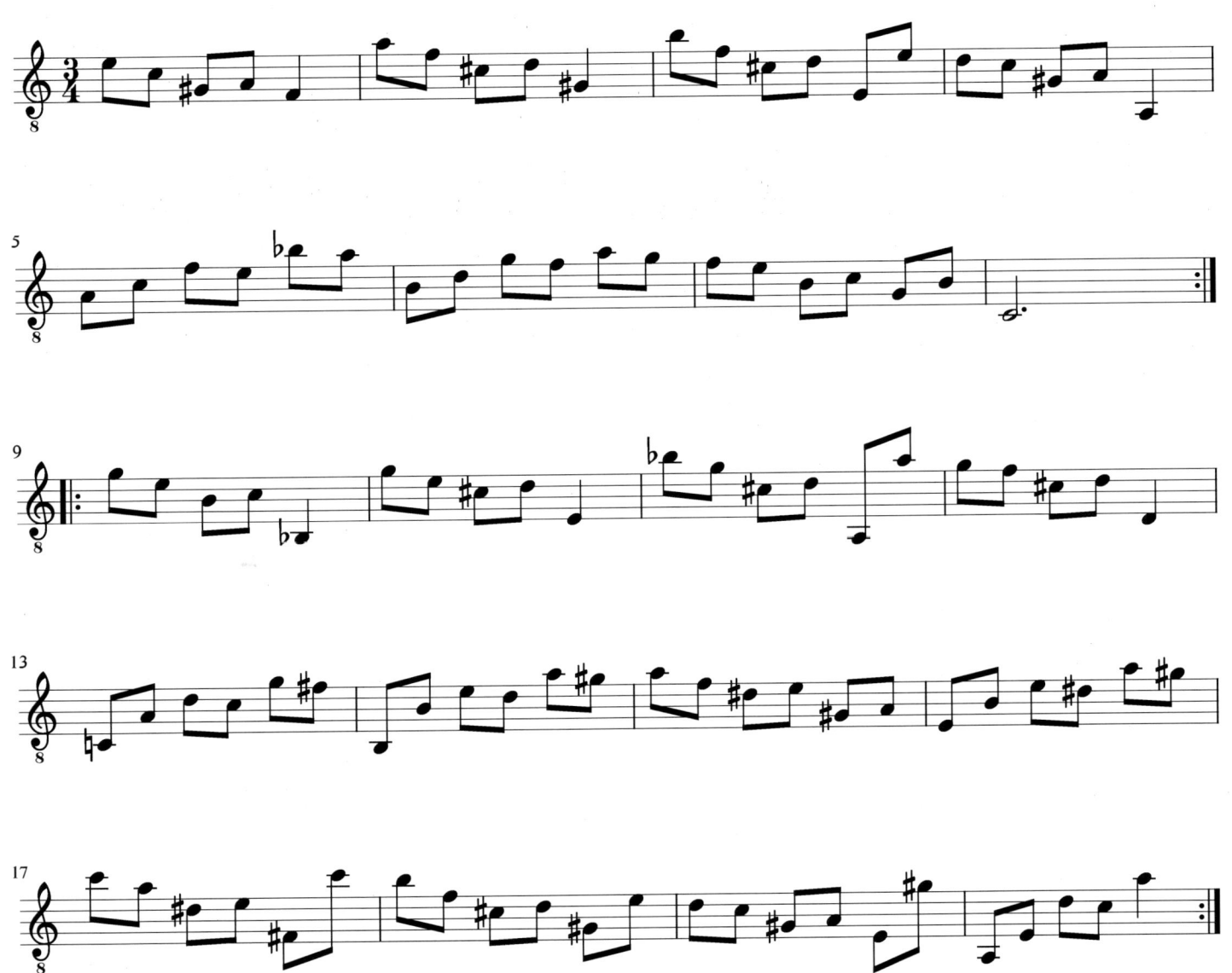

Gavotte I & II

Arranged for plectrum guitar
by Rob MacKillop

J. S. Bach

Gigue

Arranged for plectrum guitar
by Rob MacKillop

J. S. Bach

This page has been left blank to avoid an awkward page turn.

Cello Suite No. 6
Prelude

Arranged for plectrum guitar
by Rob MacKillop

J. S. Bach

Allemande

Arranged for plectrum guitar
by Rob MacKillop

J. S. Bach

Courante

Arranged for plectrum guitar
by Rob MacKillop

J. S. Bach

Sarabande

Arranged for plectrum guitar
by Rob MacKillop

J. S. Bach

This page has been left blank to avoid an awkward page turn.

Gavotte I & II

Arranged for plectrum guitar
by Rob MacKillop

J. S. Bach

Gigue

Arranged for plectrum guitar
by Rob MacKillop

J. S. Bach

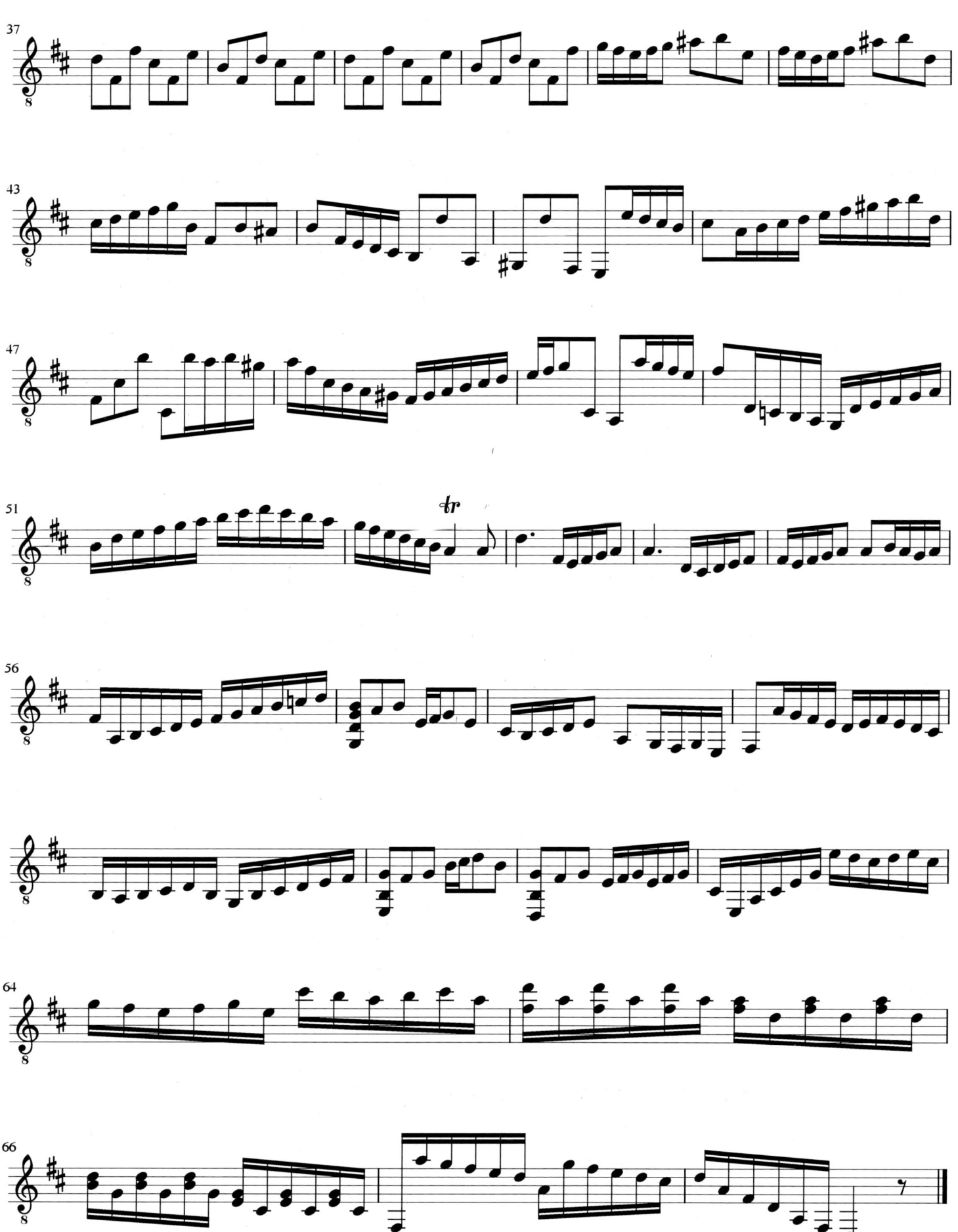

Other Mel Bay Plectrum Guitar Solo & Ensemble Books

6 Pieces for Guitar Solo (Pritchard)

13 Easy Trios for Guitar (Murdick)

24 Pieces for Guitar by Gilbert Isbin

25 Solos from the Unaccompanied Partitas of J. S. Bach (W. Bay/Leonard)

Achieving Guitar Artistry: Concert Solos (W. Bay)

Achieving Guitar Artistry: Contemporary Baroque (W. Bay)

Achieving Guitar Artistry: Linear Guitar Etudes (W. Bay)

Achieving Guitar Artistry: Lyrical Etudes (Pennanen)

Achieving Guitar Artistry: Preludes, Sonatas & Nocturnes (W. Bay)

Acoustic Guitar Portraits: Duets (W. Bay)

American Patriotic Guitar Quartets (Petersen)

Beginning Baroque for Guitar (Kiefer)

Beginning Pop/Rock Guitar Etudes (Douglass)

Christmas Guitar Portraits (Duets) (W. Bay)

Christmas Music for Electric Guitar (Kiefer)

Christmas Music for Guitar Ensemble (Miller)

Classics for Electric Guitar (Kiefer)

Classics for Flatpicking Guitar (W. Bay)

Devotion: Sacred Solos for Guitar (W. Bay)

Dirt Simple Electric Guitar Solos on Open Strings (Nier)

Easy Way Christmas Guitar Folio (M. Bay)

Electric Baroque (Kiefer)

Folio of Graded Guitar Solos (M. Bay)

Fun and Easy Solos for Guitar (Minamino)

Graded Guitar Duets (M. Bay)

Guitar Airs and Ballads (W. Bay)

Guitar Duets on Great Classic Themes (Hendrickson/Orzeck)

Guitar Images (W. Bay)

WWW.MELBAY.COM

Other Mel Bay Plectrum Guitar Solo & Ensemble Books

Guitar Meditations: Contemplative Solos (W. Bay)

Guitar Nocturnes (W. Bay)

Guitar Picking Tunes - An Early American Christmas (W. Bay)

Guitar Picking Tunes - Beautiful Airs and Ballads of the British Isles (W. Bay)

Guitar Picking Tunes - Beautiful American Airs and Ballads (W. Bay)

Guitar Picking Tunes - Blues and Jazz Guitar Jam Tunes (W. Bay)

Guitar Picking Tunes - Christmas in the British Isles (W. Bay)

Guitar Picking Tunes - Classical Gems (W. Bay)

Guitar Picking Tunes - Flatpicking Classics (Troxel)

Guitar Picking Tunes - Fun Solos to Play (W. Bay)

Guitar Picking Tunes-Jumpin' Guitar Jam Tunes (W. Bay)

Guitar Preludes (W. Bay)

Guitar Solos for Improving Technique (W. Bay)

Guitar Sonatas (W. Bay)

Guitar Tangos (W. Bay)

Lively Guitar Tunes (W. Bay)

Mastering the Guitar Duets (W. Bay/M. Christiansen)

Masters of the Plectrum Guitar (Multiple Authors)

Mozart for Electric Guitar (Kiefer)

Music from Around the World for Guitar Ensemble (Miller)

One Guitar, Many Styles (Finn)

Sal Salvadore Collection of Classic Solos for Pick-Style Guitar

Short Etudes (W. Bay)

The Christmas Gig Book for Pick-Style Guitar (Coppola)

Timeless Solos for Guitar (W. Bay)

Traditional Music of the British Isles for Electric Guitar (Berthoud)

Wedding Music for Pick-Style Guitar (Coppola)

World Music for Flatpicking Guitar Made Easy (Berthoud)

WWW.MELBAY.COM

WWW.MELBAY.COM